ISBN-13: 978-17985-95244

Text and Illustrations copyright Leo DeBroeck, 2019
No part of this publication may be reproduced in whole or in part, or stored in a retrieval system, or transmitted in any form, or by any means, electronic, mechanical, photocopying, recording, or otherwise, without written permission of the author.
All rights reserved.

About this book:

This book is intended as a tool for adults to be able to talk and process with children about the death of a loved one. Grief and loss are complicated emotions that we are not born knowing how to handle. Loss has an effect on our thoughts, emotions, and actions that needs to be processed and understood. This book models several ways to deal with grief after the death of loved one. It shows that there is strength in expressing your emotions in appropriate ways. This book models several ways to deal with grief after the death of loved one. It teaches that it is acceptable to feel sadness but to also hold onto the memory of the loved one and to continue having more memories with other loved ones. The story highlights that grief comes in waves and the difference between "moving forward" and "stuffing down" emotions. This book values holding onto your memories of the loved one while also letting go of the person through accepting your emotions. This book lightly suggests that to process grief it may help to create a physical representation of a favorite memory with them, such as a memory box or photographs.

In order to be able to help a child with death, it helps being able to talk about the purpose of life. The book identifies the value of spending meaningful quality time together with the people you love and learning life lessons along the way as some of the primary reasons of healthy relationships in life. This book does not discuss what happens to a person after death or any spiritual beliefs in order to encourage discussion and openness about these questions. It is important while reading the book together to show that you also have strong feelings of grief in your life. Through this, you model for them that they can talk about loss without overwhelming or hurting you. Present that grief is not a "problem" but a natural reaction to the loss. By discussing loss, the conversation shows that you can be emotionally present at the same time as being able to continue to care for them. Teach the child to deal with grief by showing the child how. Being strong for them means showing the child you are not afraid to allow yourself to feel grief and loss.

Dedicated to Joe and Diana Bushnell

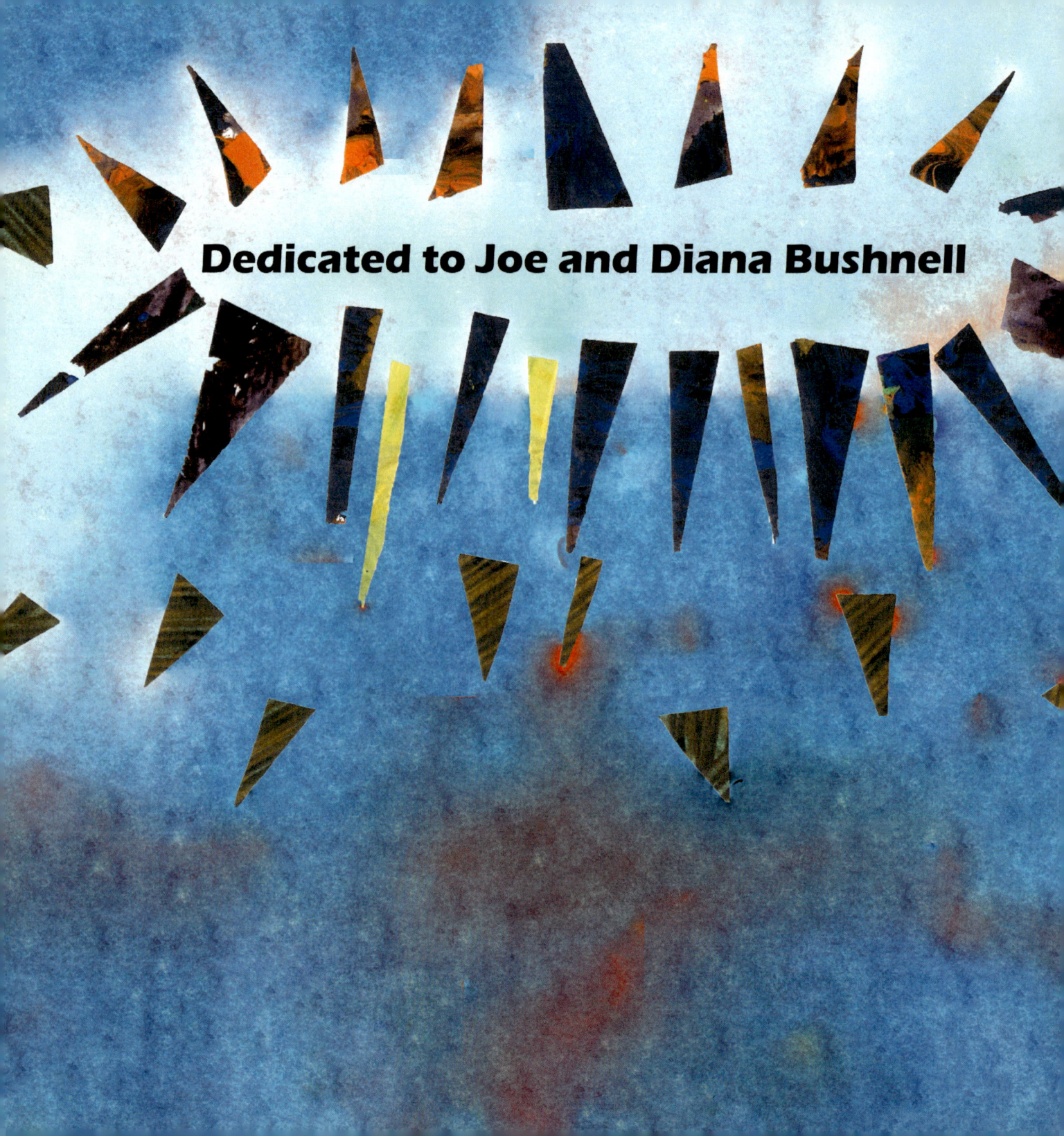

Grandpa's Circle of Life

Authored and Illustrated by:
Leo DeBroeck, MS
Licensed Mental Health Counselor

Things to know about grief with children:

Precise and simple language will help children understand without overbearing them with information. Saying, "This person has died" will lead to a better understanding and questions from the child such as, "What does that mean?" Whereas saying, "This person has left us" will lead to more confusion from the child and questions such as, "When are they going to come back?"

Kids will do what you do, not what you tell them to do. If you feel pain from the death of a loved one and do not ever show it to the child, they are not likely to open up and process the emotion with you either. You should not use your child as your emotional support but part of being their emotional support is showing them how to experience grief by:

First, allowing yourself to feel grief and meet them where they are emotionally by crying or another emotional expression.

Second, showing a way out of that "wave" of grief together with the child by talking through the different sensations in your body (e.g. My heart feels like it's really heavy), talking about the memories of the person, talking about the thoughts you have (e.g. I just wish I could see them again), and doing an activity or making something in their memory. It is not as healthy to ignore the grief or distract from it by going and doing something else during the initial "waves" of grief.

It can help to identify feelings by going through body sensations. If you tell a child to, "Tell me how you're feeling?" They typically do not know. It can help with the steps of processing to ask more simple questions, "In my heart, I feel sad like it is getting pulled out. In my eyes, I feel I want to cry. In my chest, I feel I want a hug. My throat feels like it has a knot in it and that I want to scream.

What do you feel like in your heart?... eyes?... throat?"

Grandpa's Circle of Life

Things to know about grief with children:

When children are recalling any memory, event, or person that they typically do not remember things in order. Children will automatically fill in information they do not have with imagined information. As long as they are remembering the right person this will not interfere with processing emotions. It is usually okay that this happens and does not get in the way of processing emotions.

Anger is a normal reaction for a child to have with sadness, feelings of loss, confusion, anxiety, and fear.

Children process grief differently than adults. Where adults typically grieve using ceremony, rituals, or formal scripts of words, children can process using more images, actions, or objects.

Encouraging the child to grieve and create a memorial from their memory of the one who died is recommended. Forcing the child to create something is not helpful. This can lead to many different activities:

1) Making a scrap book or "memory book" of the person
2) Going through pictures
3) Telling stories about them together
4) Going to their favorite place with the person and saying out loud good-byes to the person
5) Writing goodbye cards
6) Making a drawing
7) Planting a tree
8) Creating a comic strip
9) Writing the 'lessons' they learned from the person
10) Writing a story of the dead

Grandpa's Circle of Life

Things to know about grief with children:

Common questions to be expected when discussing grief and death are:

1) What happens after you die?
2) Where are they now?
3) Where do animals go when they die?
4) Was it my fault or was it because of me?
5) Is it okay if I do not cry?
6) If it does not hurt, does it mean I did not love them?
7) What will (family event/holiday) be like without them?
8) Does their body still feel pain or need to breathe?
9) Will I die someday?
10) Will you die someday or when will you die?
11) Should I be worried about dying or losing you?
12) Does it hurt to die?
13) What happens to my body when I die?
14) Can they still see me?
15) If I die, will I be able to see them again?
16) When I dream about them, is that because they came and visited me?
17) What happens if I forget everything about them and cannot remember them anymore?
18) Why do people die?
19) Does grief always "hit" right away?
20) What happens when everyone who remembers me dies?
21) What happens to my memories of others when I die?

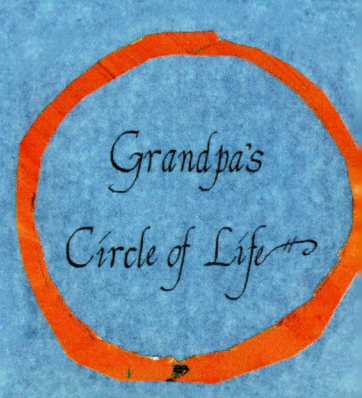

Grandpa's Circle of Life

Grandpa's Circle of Life

Not too long ago, my family and I were going to visit the beach. This made me feel sick in my stomach, sad, and happy, all at the same time. The smell of salt water, the seagulls, circular fire pits, all of it made me feel this way. It reminded me of someone I love a lot and something they taught me.

This is the story of my grandpa and I at the ocean. After a long year of school, it is finally summer! My family would drive all day to the ocean for the summer. My grandpa and grandma lived there. My grandpa and I would build castles every day for what seemed to be endless days. We would roast marshmallows over a fire, tell jokes, play in the water, and have more fun during one day than any other person could have in a lifetime.

First, the drive to the ocean is always really long, but with so much to see, I can't fall asleep. We go past gigantic skyscrapers in the city so tall you can't see the top. Then, we go through the small and calm trees by the road and see blue birds that have not a single reason to hurry. Nothing in the world seemed happier than those blue birds, except maybe me because I am going to see my grandpa.

After the drive, we finally arrive at our grandparents' home. The smell of fresh growing vegetables, the thriving plants in a warm green house, and grandma's tasty cooking. I feel the air just beginning to warm my face or maybe that is my excitement! It is the happy feeling of a brand new summer that is about to start.

I go up to the door and swing it right open. Suddenly, I hear the funny sound of a rubber dancing fish, "Don't worry, be happy, every little thing is going to be alright." My good'ol grandpa sitting in front of the TV says, "What took you so long? I've been waiting for you all year!" I'd reply, "School!"

Funny Fish

Next, grandma says, "Come over here and give your grandma a hug!" Her arms are wide open for her hug. Faster than lightning grandpa is outside with his walking stick and a small shovel ready to leave for the beach to build sand castles. Our favorite thing to do together.

My grandpa is great. He had thick black hair, large ears, and more liver spots than anyone I've ever seen. He had soft blue eyes, big strong fingers, and a bulky nose. He loved to play games with me, play with kites, play catch, play cards, play old music, and every other kind of "play" you can think of. That is until it was nap time. He liked to take naps too.

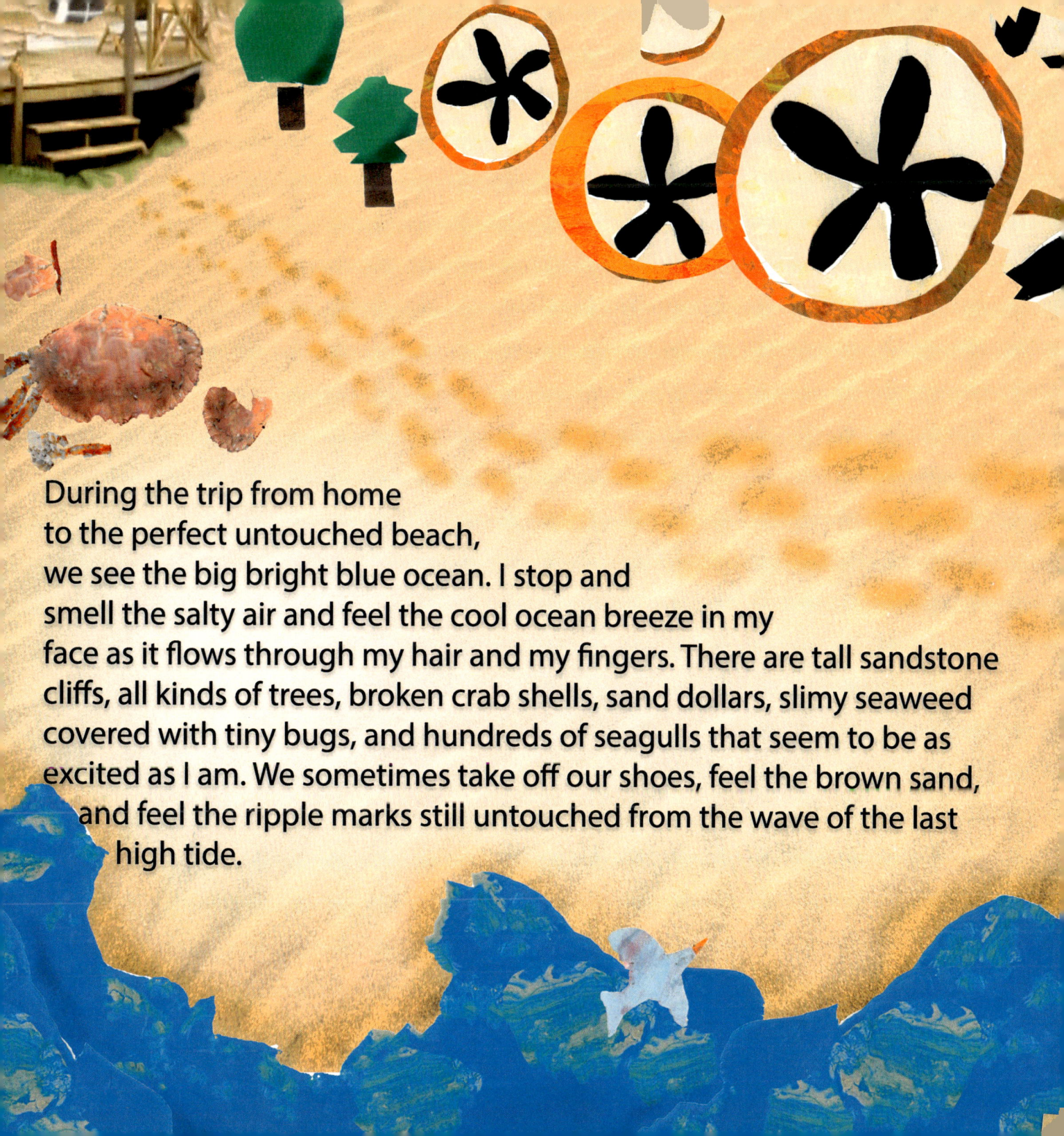

During the trip from home
to the perfect untouched beach,
we see the big bright blue ocean. I stop and
smell the salty air and feel the cool ocean breeze in my
face as it flows through my hair and my fingers. There are tall sandstone
cliffs, all kinds of trees, broken crab shells, sand dollars, slimy seaweed
covered with tiny bugs, and hundreds of seagulls that seem to be as
excited as I am. We sometimes take off our shoes, feel the brown sand,
and feel the ripple marks still untouched from the wave of the last
high tide.

At first, we just listen to the ocean waves. It sounds gentle and peaceful. As we got closer and closer to the water, the sea mist in the air feels cooling like you could touch it! The warm breeze tickles my skin and seems to freeze time. There was no spot in the world that is more calm and relaxed. This is my favorite memory with my grandpa.

Near the water at the beautiful beach, we grab our shovels and dig together. We make a moat in a large circle with a big tower in the middle. The sandcastle in the center of the circle got bigger and bigger. My grandpa tells me, "Everything goes in a circle. Not always a perfect circle but still close enough." I tell him that I don't understand. He just let me know that I would one day. Life was perfect and it felt like it would never change.

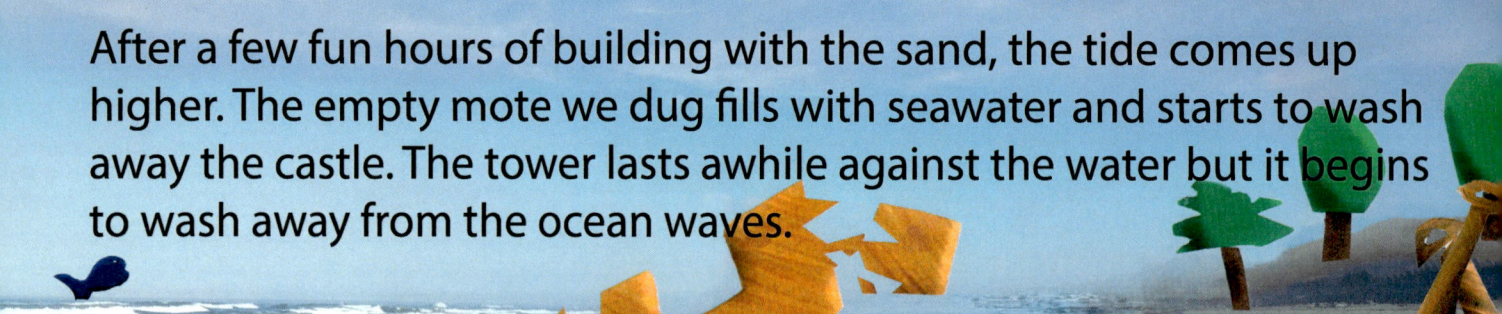

After a few fun hours of building with the sand, the tide comes up higher. The empty mote we dug fills with seawater and starts to wash away the castle. The tower lasts awhile against the water but it begins to wash away from the ocean waves.

Even though the castle is surrounded by water, it still takes a long time to go back to nothing but flat sand again. My grandpa says to me, "It started out as nothing. Like a circle it will go back to how it started. Between starting as nothing and ending as nothing, we made something important together. We made a happy memory together that will always last. The castle will be gone soon but we can always remember the time we spent together making it."

After the sandcastle, we go looking for sand dollars on the beach. Grandpa shows me a sand dollar and says, "This sand dollar shows where it is in life. Its life goes in a circle from sand to this full dollar and then back to nothing but sand again. That is what I call the circle of life." Then from the ground, he picks out some brown sand and another sand dollar that was broken into pieces.

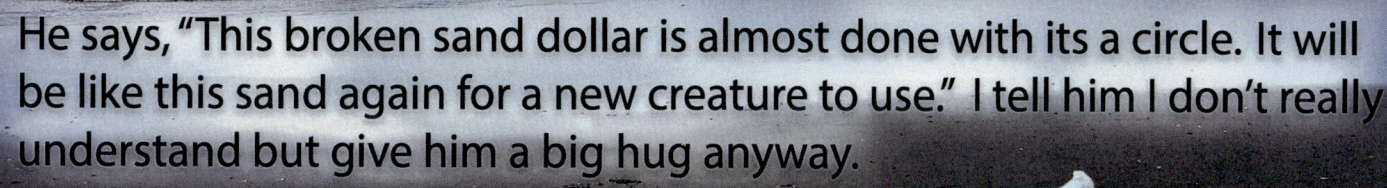

He says, "This broken sand dollar is almost done with its a circle. It will be like this sand again for a new creature to use." I tell him I don't really understand but give him a big hug anyway.

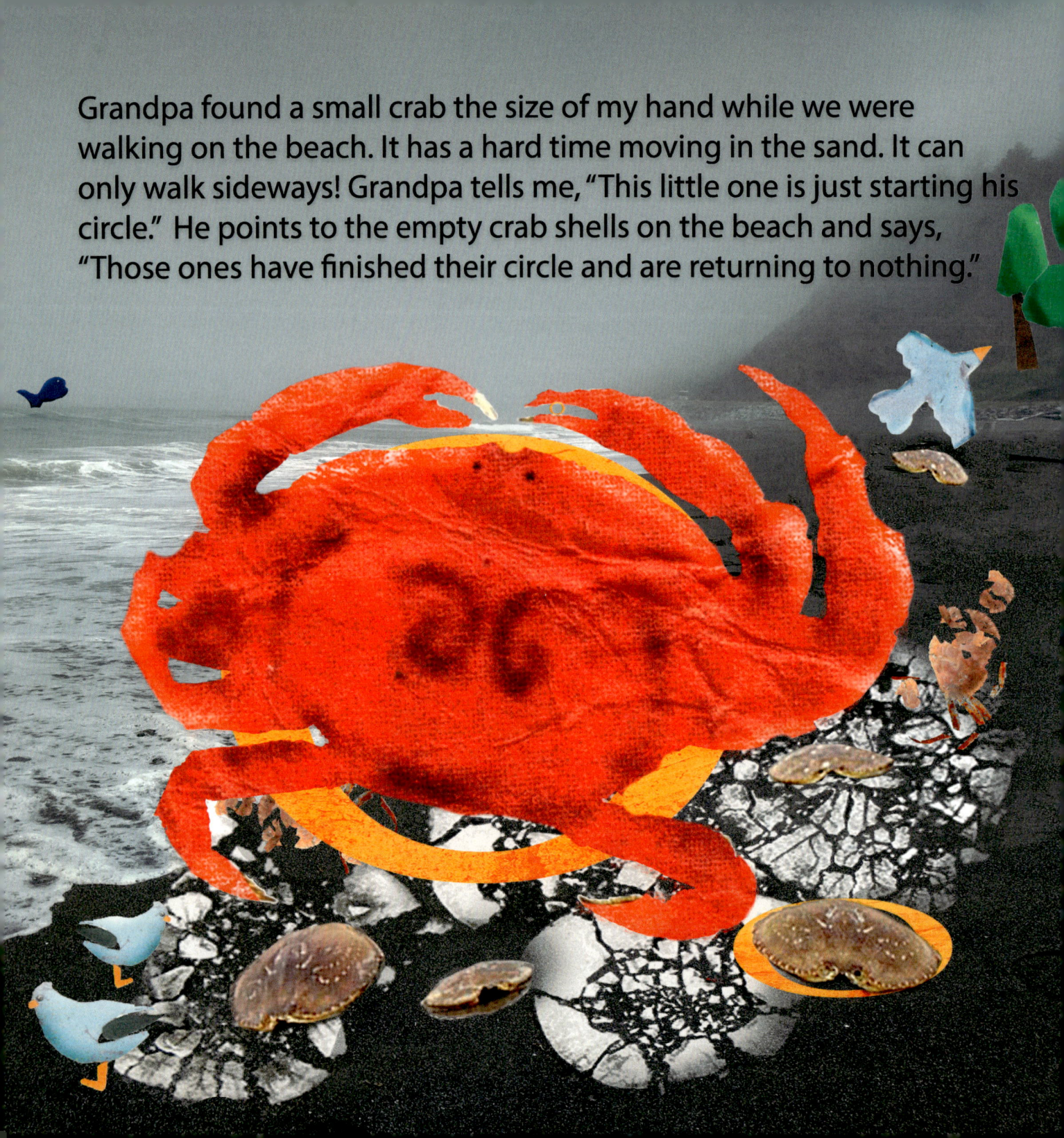

Grandpa found a small crab the size of my hand while we were walking on the beach. It has a hard time moving in the sand. It can only walk sideways! Grandpa tells me, "This little one is just starting his circle." He points to the empty crab shells on the beach and says, "Those ones have finished their circle and are returning to nothing."

With the sandcastle almost gone, the sun starts to go down. We get our firewood and start a small campfire as we tell jokes and stories. Grandpa always tells the funniest ones. We have hot chocolate, chocolate bars, graham crackers, and roasted golden marshmallow. With my grandpa there, it was a great memory. Life could not get any better.

The sun melts away into the ocean and I asked my grandpa, "Is the day like a circle too? It starts out with so many possible memories to make and it always ends." My grandpa said, "I guess it really is a circle too." I felt full and proud of myself because I was starting to understand.

Once the castle was gone, grandpa tells me, "You cannot even tell that the castle was there anymore. It went in a full circle from nothing to its full existence then back to nothing. All things in life go in a circle." That's when he gave me the best hug ever. It was a great memory we made together.

After summer had finished its circle and come and gone, I went back home to the city and started school again. One day, I got a terrible phone call. My grandpa was sick in the hospital and was going to die. The doctors could not do anything about it.

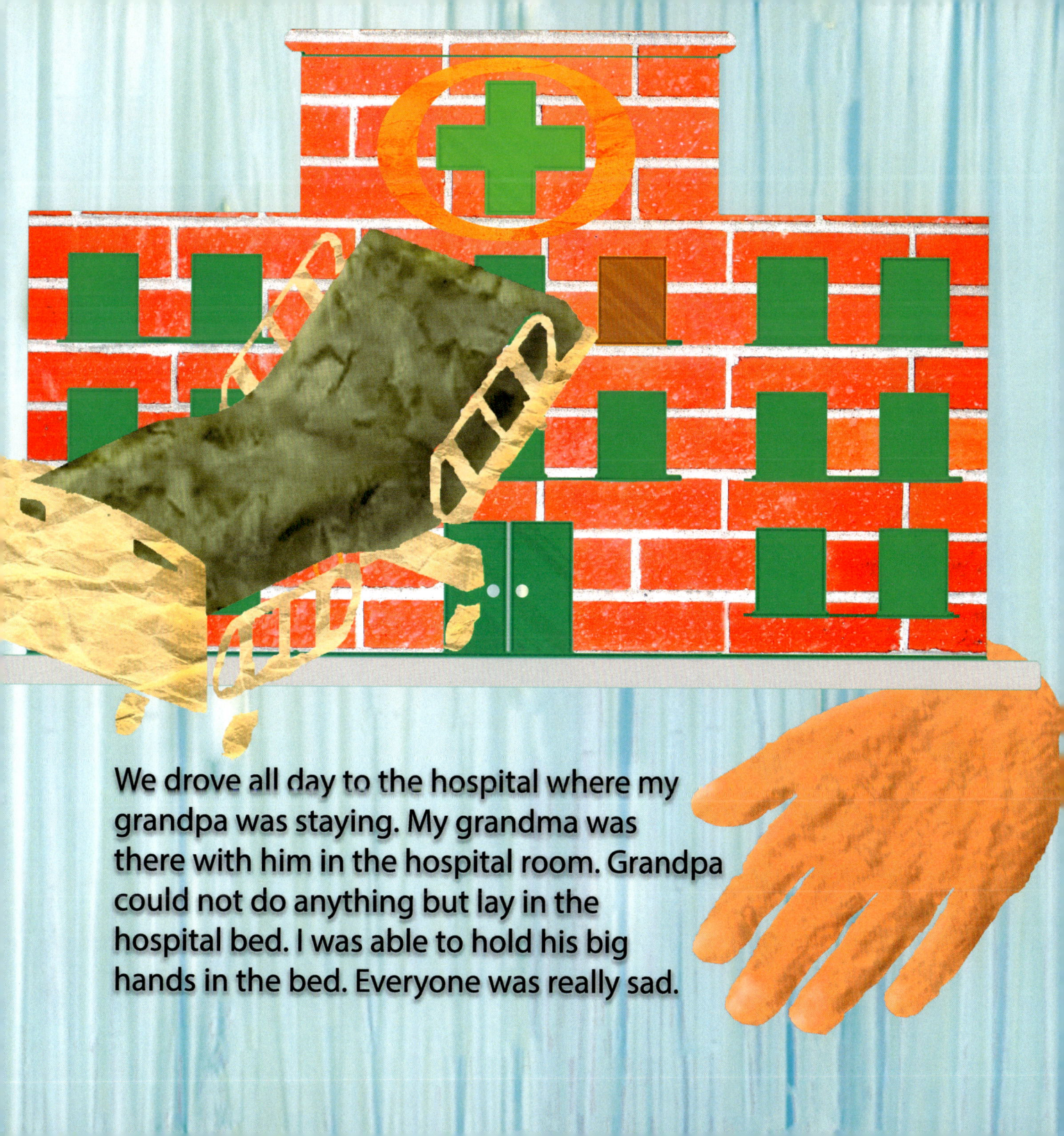

We drove all day to the hospital where my grandpa was staying. My grandma was there with him in the hospital room. Grandpa could not do anything but lay in the hospital bed. I was able to hold his big hands in the bed. Everyone was really sad.

Grandpa Joe Bushnell

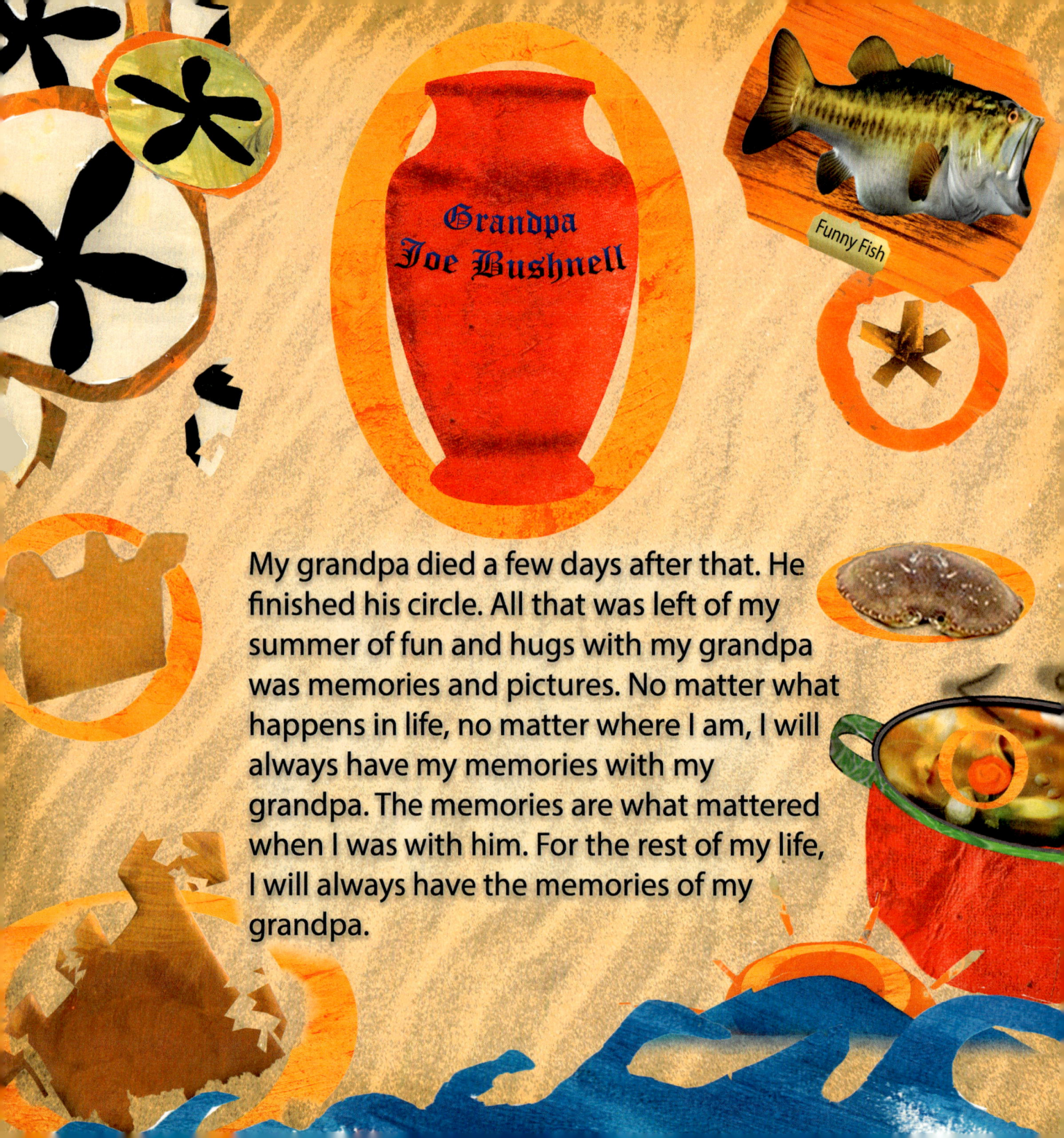

Funny Fish

My grandpa died a few days after that. He finished his circle. All that was left of my summer of fun and hugs with my grandpa was memories and pictures. No matter what happens in life, no matter where I am, I will always have my memories with my grandpa. The memories are what mattered when I was with him. For the rest of my life, I will always have the memories of my grandpa.

Now I am back at the beach with my family. Everyone there is happy and sad like me. Some people tell stories and their memories of my grandpa. Some people cry and laugh. It feels like an ocean wave is crushing my insides and I want to cry. My grandma gives me a hug and tells me, "It is okay to be sad that he's gone. It is okay to be happy he was here. You made memories with him while he was here and that is what is important."

We spread grandpa's ashes out across the ocean beach. He had finished his circle. He started out a kid just like me. He became a good person and lived a life full of memories and stories. Now he has gone back to nothing again but the memories are still shared by the people he was with, like me.

I still miss my grandpa and wish he could be with me. Sometimes it feels like an ocean wave of sadness comes back over me and I miss him all over again. The waves of feeling grief and sadness come up when something reminds me of him. It is okay that I miss him and feel that way because it makes me remember it is important to love and make more good memories with the people who care about me. Things feel better when I tell my family how I feel.

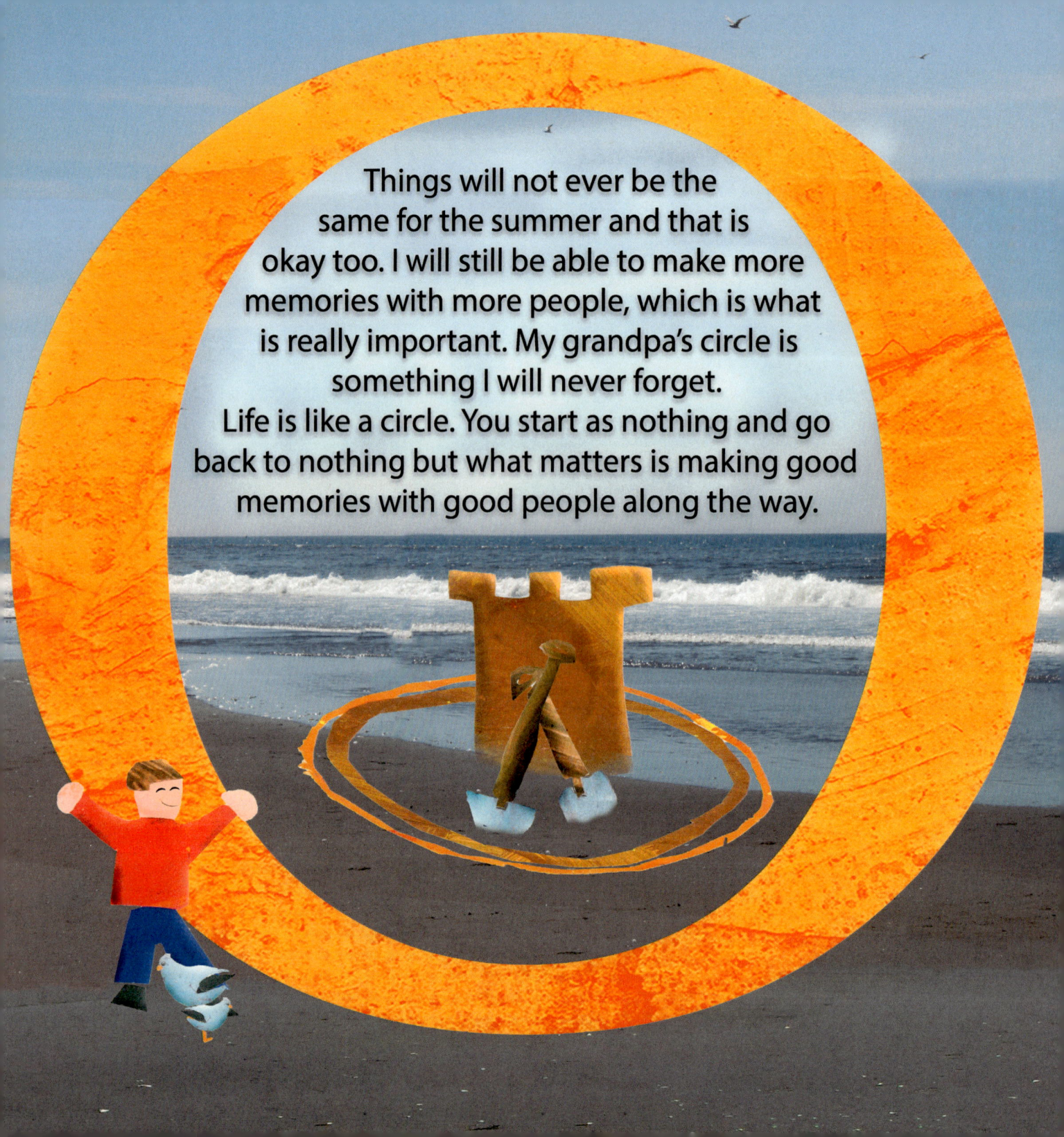

Things will not ever be the same for the summer and that is okay too. I will still be able to make more memories with more people, which is what is really important. My grandpa's circle is something I will never forget.
Life is like a circle. You start as nothing and go back to nothing but what matters is making good memories with good people along the way.

Made in the USA
Columbia, SC
26 March 2019